Stress is

The Scientific Solution:
4 Simple Steps to Reduce Stress,
Declutter Your Mind,
Conquer Overwhelm &
Reclaim Your Inner Peace

by

Prof. Dr. Detlef Beeker

http://detlefbeeker.de/en

Prof. Dr. Detlef Beeker
Happiness Researcher

Contents

Free Gift

"The clearest sign of wisdom is a consistently good mood." — Michel de Montaigne

As a thank you, I would like to give you a gift! Here's my book **"18 Surprising Good-Mood Tips"** (52 pages). You can download it at the following link:

http://detlefbeeker.de/gift/

Do you remember the first time you fell in love? Wasn't everything suddenly nice? How wonderful the blue sky looked, with its white clouds. Even rain you could enjoy. What if you could have this lovely mood all the time?

In this book, you will learn:

- **Body parts** to press to relieve stress and improve your mood and health

- Proven mental tactics that will put you in a **good mood in seconds**

- **Secret Yoga techniques** that will easily increase your good mood

- The **unknown piece of music** is scientifically proven to be the best stress reducer

- What you can learn from **James Bond** and how it gives you relaxation and self-confidence

- How you can relax in **10 seconds**

- Practice this **mind-boggling technique** and get fresh and vitalized.

- The **best apps** to relieve your stress and give you relaxation and serenity

- The **Fidget Cube** and how it works

- Bonus: The **new generation** of good mood techniques

- ... and much more

Download this book NOW for **free,** so that you'll

be guaranteed more joy, serenity, and happiness with the help of the best techniques.

http://detlefbeeker.de/gift/

About the Author

"The universe is friendly."

Amazon best-selling author Prof. Dr. Detlef Beeker is a happiness researcher and anti-stress expert. He has been researching these fields for more than 20 years and has written numerous books. Detlef is not just an author but also someone who practices what he writes. He has been meditating for more than 20 years.

Too many self-help guides give you big ideas but fail to show you how they are actually applicable. In his books, Detlef Beeker offers practical methods and step-by-step instructions that you can implement immediately.

At the age of 7, Dr. Beeker had already found his destiny. "I want to become a taster in a pudding factory," he told his mum. Although his vocation has changed since then, his deep desire to make the world a better place has remained.

Visit his website http://detlefbeeker.de/en to find lots of helpful tips, tricks, and a gift for you!

Introduction

"We all have the power to be happy in all circumstances." — Byron Katie

In this chapter...

- What you will learn in this book

- What makes this book unique

- The high-impact approach and cherry picking

Do you want to know a secret about me? However, it has to stay between us. Are you sure you want to know? It will turn your world upside down. Ok, here it comes. Hold on tight.

My brain is still from the Stone Age. It is about 135,000 years old!

It's from a time when we were hunted by tigers and lived in caves. By the way, your brain is too.

The fact that I have a Stone Age brain is annoying, and I say that quite openly. It is the root of all stress. Our brains are an ingenious bio-computer programmed to survive. And that is exactly what causes our stress. Why? You will learn this in the first chapter.

Stress is omnipresent. Modern brain research

knows exactly how stress runs in the brain and what the causes are. We can use this knowledge to tackle stress at the root. We fight not only the symptoms but also the true causes. The amazing thing is that you can apply a few simple techniques to overcome stress at any time without much effort.

In this book, you will discover

- A simple technique used by modern psychotherapists and ancient Greek philosophers to prevent stress

- How to resolve stress, worry, and anxiety in seconds with a scientifically proven technique

- Learn the secret SSBB technique that lets you relax in 20 seconds, even when your boss is bugging you

- How to turn stress into strength and energy with a simple trick

- Why advice from counselors often does not work, and the wisdom of cutting-edge brain research is the key to eradicating stress

- Bonus: The most efficient productivity hacks to keep you on the ball

- Bonus: The best nutritional supplements and herbal remedies that help you effortlessly reduce your stress

What's different about this book

Most stress experts tell you what you can do differently on the outside. You can clear your house, quit your job, improve your relationship, and/or delegate your work. These are very helpful tips, but they do not address the real reasons. This book grabs the stress at the root.

The Dalai Lama has a busy schedule. He rushes from one appointment to the next. Is he stressed because of that? No! Why? Because stress is largely not dependent on external factors, but how we handle them. About 2000 years ago, the former slave and great philosopher Epictetus realized:

It is not the things themselves that disturb us, but rather the ideas and opinions of things.

We will discuss this in detail later in the book. I'll give you efficient tools on how to do it. A small spoiler – it's not difficult at all!

Another special feature of this book is that we use findings of modern brain research. Researchers have found that the main contributors to the body's stress response are the amygdala and the prefrontal cortex. In the next chapter, this will be explained in detail. When we understand how these two organs act, we can fight stress more efficiently. We use this kind of knowledge in this book so that you can really reduce your stress.

The high-impact approach

Would you like to find out another secret? This time it's nothing world-shaking.

I have no time!

I work full-time as a professor, I have a family, and I write books. Incidentally, I do not just write, but I read, no, I devour books! I love non-fiction, guidebooks, science fiction, and fantasy books. Since I read many non-fiction and reference books for work, I am one of those who wants to get to the point quickly. I like it when the information in a book is easily accessible. It bothers me if the information is hidden in page-long flow texts or stories.

It's like having a huge loaf of white bread a meter in diameter. In the middle of this gigantic loaf of bread is a raisin. You have to fight your way through the layers of bread until you can finally eat the one raisin. This book, on the other hand, is a small, handy bun with many raisins! With every delicious bite, you will get at least one of the delicious raisins!

Since I want to make the reading experience as pleasant as possible for you, I have designed this book to be **user-friendly**.

- **Straight to the point**: I eliminated everything that inflated the text artificially. The language is relaxed. The topic "stress" is already hard enough.

- **Bullet points:** In this book, you will find many bullet points. Everything is easily accessible and is not hidden in long-running texts.

- **Introductory reviews, summary, and other tips to make your life easier:** Let's say that you are in a strange city and you are looking for the train station. There are leading you to the station, but in one turn, a sign is missing. You cannot find the station. This book is like a very friendly city. There are signs everywhere. Everyone knows where he is and where to go.

- **Structuring**: This book is very structured with many sub-chapters so that the important information is quickly accessible.

I call this the High-Impact Approach, because the information density in this book is very high and at the same time, all information is clearly accessible: You do not have to look far, and you do not have to dig in the ground! Rather, I'll hand you the golden nuggets on a silver platter.

Ready? Let's continue with Chapter 1.

In a Nutshell

- Our brain has not changed significantly in the last 135,000 years. We all have a Stone Age brain in our skull. This is responsible for our stress.

- If we look at stress from the brain's point of view, the main participants are the amygdala and the prefrontal cortex. Between you and me, the amygdala is the real culprit.

- Rather than the actual events being responsible for our stress, it is instead our reactions. That's why the Dalai Lama is not stressed.

- This book has a High-Impact Approach. That means that all information is very easily accessible. Stories and other stuff that inflates the book artificially are eliminated as much as possible.

Chapter One
Stress from the point of view
of the brain

*"It is not the amount of work that causes
everyday stress, but the person who criticizes
and presses you for it. Admittedly, sometimes
you are that person."* — Peter Hohl

In this chapter...

- What is stress?

- Why is stress an illusion?

- Stress does not have to be real

- How does stress in the brain work?

- Why are the amygdala and the prefrontal
cortex the main actors?

- How exactly do we best beat stress?

Modern life is stressful. There are many challenges that can easily become overburdening.
You may care for a baby, you may be at risk of
unemployment, or you may have a new, de-
manding job. Stress can arise because you have
separated from or lost someone. It may be that
your body is aging, you have a chronic illness, or
have become overweight. Stressful can also be a

disharmonious relationship or financial problems. You carry an unresolved trauma from your childhood, and this is causing you stress. There are countless possibilities that can trigger stress.

Stress *is defined as a real or perceived threat to our body or ego.*

It may be that a tiger chases us or the feeling of helplessness plagues us. Both trigger stress. An interesting aspect of the definition is that stress can also be triggered by non-real hazards. It depends on the perception. James Bond has a different perception of danger than Mr. Bean did. For stress to be triggered, we only have to *perceive* something as a danger. Whether it is real or not is secondary. Often the biggest stressors are not people or things, but instead are our thoughts. Making a speech is not a real danger, but this situation can still cause stress.

How do you know when you are stressed? Stress has three main features.

- **Flat Breathing**. Stress and anxiety make us breathe "flatter" and faster. We breathe flat in the ribcage instead of deep into the stomach. This increases the stress, and we breathe even flatter. This can lead to a cycle that increases our stress.

- **Physical tension**. When we are under stress, we get tense. After a hard day at work, you may have a headache. This arises because you tense and cramp up. This often happens unconsciously. Observe yourself. If you have a quarrel with your partner, you involuntarily contract your back and neck muscles. Stress is always accompanied by physical tension.

- **Narrowed perception**. In cases of stress and anxiety, we get tunnel vision. This comes from the Stone Age. When we were in danger, our perception narrowed, and we focused on fight, flight, or freeze. Our perception narrowed. This has been preserved to this day.

We can use these features purposefully. For example, we can consciously breathe deeply in stressful situations. This helps dissolve stress quickly. Later we'll talk about other very effective anti-stress techniques.

Whether you suffer from stress, you know yourself best.

Nevertheless, I recommend the following two stress tests.

https://www.bemindfulonline.com/test-your-stress/ This test is done quickly. You get a good first impression about your stress level.

http://www.mentalhealthamerica.net/stress-screener This test is detailed. You answer a lot of questions, but it's scientifically proven and gives you reliable information.

Stress is just an Illusion

"Stress is an illusion" is a bold statement. How did I hit on that? Stress is real! We feel the tension of our body and the shallow breathing. That's no illusion! You are right and wrong. Let me explain it:

Our brain is that of our ancestors. Their lives were hard and very dangerous: hunger, harsh environmental conditions and predators were a constant danger. The better our brain was able to cope with these environmental conditions, the higher the chance of survival. So our brain is specialized in surviving. It is a survival expert. How do you survive? By recognizing dangers early. Over many millennia, this ability has been steadily improved because it was essential to our survival. That's why today we have a brain that is an expert in hazard detection. At the same time, the brain was cautious. Situations were classified as a danger in case of doubt. Rather consider a safe situation to be dangerous than to overlook a threat.

Our world today is comparatively harmless. We don't have to be careful every moment that a tiger is behind us. We do not have to worry about starving. Our dangers today are, for example, high blood pressure or diabetes. To be clear, we have a Stone Age brain that lives in a modern world. Because of this, many situations are considered a threat by our brains, although they are harmless to our survival. In the past, danger meant we either had to flee or fight. If we have an appointment but are stuck in a traffic jam, that does not really threaten our lives. However, our brain considers this a danger. That is the point. There is no danger, but our brain rates it as such. If we have an unpleasant conversation with our partner, it does not threaten our lives, and we do not have to flee or fight. The danger is an illusion. Our Stone Age brain sees a mortal danger that is not there. By our definition, stress is a real or perceived threat. However, this threat does not really exist. So stress is just an illusion.

In brief: *The stress reaction of our body protected us from immediate, physical dangers, like a tiger attack. It was vital to our survival. In today's world, our Stone Age brain still sees life-threatening dangers everywhere. A dissatisfied*

*customer or being stuck in traffic jams are no
danger. They're just an illusion.*

I hope I've convinced you that stress is indeed an
illusion. This is particularly important for the
long-term fight against stress. Now, let's take a
look at our alarm system.

The amygdala:
The overzealous alarm system

Let's take a closer look: The amygdala is responsible for recognizing dangers in our brain. This is
the alarm system of our brain. It's about in the
middle of our head. The amygdala is a little over
a centimeter in size and is the shape of two al-
monds.

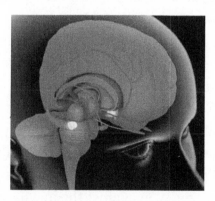

Quelle: http://tinyurl.com/ycevo248.

*Imagine your Stone Age ancestor, Fred, taking
a digestive walk. Suddenly he hears a noise.*

Danger! It's a hyena. Once the amygdala detects
a danger, everything happens in a flash. Glu-
cose and adrenaline are released, our heart
beats faster and our blood is pumped to our
muscles. Our body is prepared for flight or fight
at breathtaking speed. A fast automatic reaction
was of utmost importance for our survival.
Emotionally this means that if the body is ready
to flee, we feel fear. If we fight, we feel rage.
Fred has a choice: He can run away from the
hyena or he fights. But he doesn't really have a
choice: The processes run automatically. Fred
will either feel fear and run away or he will feel
great anger and fight the hyena.

There is a third possibility besides fighting or
fleeing, namely "to freeze." Imagine you are in
the middle of a road. A car's coming your way.
You no longer have the opportunity to step aside.
That means fighting or escaping are no longer
options. Your body freezes. Your heart rate slows
down, your breathing flattens out, and your
whole system shuts down. You may feel dizzy or
even lose consciousness. All this has the function
of desensitizing you against the inevitable pain.
So your body is arming itself against unavoidable
pain. This process is called "freeze" and is one of
the possible stress reactions.

*In brief: The **amygdala** is the alarm system of our body. If you recognize a danger, your body will be prepared to fight, flee, or freeze in a flash. These are the stress reactions of the body.*

Prefrontal cortex: the thinker

The prefrontal cortex is the manager of the brain. It sets the tone and directs the brain. The prefrontal cortex is located at the front of the brain.

Prefrontal Cortex

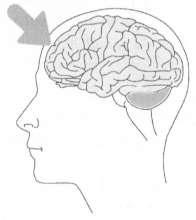

It evaluates the current stress situation and links it to past experiences. The prefrontal cortex can be our friend in solving stressful situations: It...

- solves difficult situations
- controls our impulses

- calms intense feelings

- directs our attention

- adapts to uncertain and challenging situations

The prefrontal cortex prevents us from yelling at our little child because he or she does not want to put on a coat. It reminds us that we want to be good and loving parents. The prefrontal cortex prevents us from throwing our notebook out of the window because something is not working again. It motivates us to go out for a jog instead of watching our favorite show and eating chocolate ice cream.

The prefrontal cortex is connected to the amygdala and can have a calming effect on it. Stress is a reaction that involves the whole body. However, we are focusing on the interaction between the amygdala and prefrontal cortex. That's enough for our anti-stress strategy.

In brief*: The amygdala is the alarm system, the prefrontal cortex the managing director. It can have a calming effect on the amygdala and is our ally in dealing with stress.*

Why are even smaller things, such as traffic jams, experienced as stress?

In animals, many stress triggers are present from birth. A foal can identify a predator shortly after birth and flee. This is different from people. We learn from our environment what is dangerous and what is not. This process is completed within about seven years. This does not mean that the brain cannot be changed afterwards, but a lot is invested in these years. That's why humans are incredibly adaptable. They can find their way around in many different environments with different dangers. Let's look at an example of what this has to do with stress.

Joe didn't have an easy childhood. His mother changed jobs frequently. They were always in financial straits. He studied and earned his master's degree. Joe found a good job in a reputable company. This company merged with another company. Since then, Joe has been worried. He fears for his job. Rationally, he has nothing to worry about. He had saved a lot and is very good in his field. It would be easy for him to find a new job. Nevertheless, this situation stressed him. This was caused by his childhood. He was conditioned that life was insecure. A person can lose their job quickly, and this was a dangerous situation for Joe. That's why his amygdala judged Joe's current job situation frightening. That put Joe on constant alert. His prefrontal cortex was unable to calm the amygdala.[2]

Joe's childhood was the reason for his later stress reactions. It doesn't always have to be childhood experiences, but later experiences can also trigger stress. For example, if you have a car accident, this can cause stress later in similar situations.

Chronic stress

Acute stress does not always have to be negative. If we have to make a speech, it can be a stressful situation for many people. This means that our heart rate increases, our blood pressure rises, and glucose is released. This can be positive for a speech. We are motivated and attentive. We do our best. Chronic stress, on the other hand, is unhealthy. It is caused by long-lasting stress, through, for example, a conflict-laden relationship or stressful work. Chronic stress leads to obesity, high blood pressure, and other diseases. In this book you will learn how to reduce acute and chronic stress.

A simple strategy solves your stress

Stress is a game between the amygdala and pre-frontal cortex. The prefrontal cortex has a direct connection to the amygdala. There is an analogy to this.

The amygdala is the overzealous personal bodyguard who protects a VIP. The overzealous bodyguard shoots at anything that moves. The prefrontal cortex is head of security. It has two tasks.

- In the acute situation, the boss calms the bodyguards so that they stop shooting.

- If no stress situation is present, the boss teaches the bodyguards that they should not shoot at everything, but instead only at really dangerous assassins.

There goes the analogy. It outlines our strategy against stress very well. In this book, you will learn how to...

- **Reduce acute stress reaction**

You will learn techniques that you can use when you are in the middle of a stressful situation. These techniques can quickly get you feeling less stressed. This is addressed in Chapter 2.

- **Get to the root of the stress problem**

In chapter 3, you will learn how to prevent stressful reactions from occurring. The number of situations considered dangerous is reduced. The amygdala does not sound a constant alarm, but only when there is a real danger in your life. It is therefore adapted to modern life. We achieve this by using the enormous capacities of the prefrontal cortex. It can analyze situations and solve problems. We use our analytical skills. So it is a question of changing our thoughts in order to assess situations differently.

In a Nutshell

- Stress is defined as a real or perceived threat to our body or ego.

- Stress is often caused by imaginary dangers.

- The amygdala triggers the stress reactions of "flight, fight, or freeze."

- The prefrontal cortex is our friend. With its help, we can reduce our stress.

Chapter Two
Instant relief from stress:
Calming the amygdala

"My brain is my second most important organ." — Woody Allen

In this chapter...

- How best to deal with an acute stress reaction

- A particularly effective breathing technique, 4-7-8-breathing

- In the here and now through SSBB technique

The amygdala, our personal protection, triggers the stress reaction "flight-fight-freeze" when there are signs of danger. Formerly vital, nowadays it is often inappropriate. Stress hormones such as adrenalin and cortisol are released, and we are flooded with stressful thoughts and intense feelings occur. This is not helpful when we are having discussions with our boss.

"If I only had to choose one technique to deal with stress, I would choose mindfulness." — Dr. Melanie Greenberg

Mindfulness is the antipode to stress. Mindfulness takes you to a distance away from your thoughts. You no longer will feel laden by your anxious and stressful thoughts. Mindfulness calms the feelings, the stress reaction is relieved, and the body can relax. A great tool for mindfulness is **meditation**. It has been proven by countless studies that meditation has many positive effects on body and mind. Among other things, meditation is an excellent way to relieve stress. In my book ***Bet I Can Make You Happy,*** I dedicated a whole chapter to meditation. There you will learn a particularly effective and effortless form of meditation. Alternatively, there are many good tutorials on YouTube. The problem with meditation is that it is often not sustained. We Westerners are used to things being hectic and stressful, so it is not easy for us to sit still and turn our attention inwards. For this reason, I have refrained from meditation here and offer two other techniques in this chapter that can be performed anytime and anywhere. They have similar effects to meditation but are much shorter.

In this chapter, you will learn how to deal with an already triggered stress reaction. You will learn two very effective techniques that will quickly get you out of the stress reaction.

How to resolve worries, fears, and stress in seconds

The following breathing technique has been propagated by Dr. Weil. It is surprisingly effective and helps against anxiety and panic better than any medication.[1]

4-7-8-Breath

Goal: Relaxation

Technique

1. With the tip of your tongue, touch your palate just behind your upper incisors. Leave your tongue in this position throughout the entire breathing.

2. Breathe out completely through your mouth and lips, with a whoosh sound, like you want to blow out your candles on the birthday cake.

3. Close your mouth and inhale silently through your nose, counting to four.

4. Hold your breath, counting to seven.

---

[1] Weil: *Spontaneous Happiness: Step-by-Step to peak emotional wellbeing*, 2011.

5. Breathe out through your mouth as described under point two, counting to eight.

6. Repeat steps three, four, and five for a total of four breaths.

How often? How long? At least twice a day. And every time you feel stressed. Do not take more than four breaths for the first four weeks. After that you are welcome to do more.

Tips & Tricks

- **Effective against stress and anxiety:** This breathing technique was propagated by Dr. Andrew Weil. It's a great remedy for anxiety and stress. Performed daily, this respiration also has other positive effects, such as a significant drop in blood pressure or a lowering of the average heart rate. This breathing technique is so effective that it works even better against anxiety and panic attacks than drugs. It is a simple and very effective, relaxing, breathing technique.

- **Video:** Dr. Weil explains the breathing technique in a video under the following link: http://tinyurl.com/4-7-8.

- **Tips to keep the ball rolling** can be

found in the chapter "Bonus: How to stay tuned".

You can use the 4-7-8-Breath at any time. It works quickly. Try it out. By the way, if you can't sleep, the 4-7-8-Breath helps very much. In the next chapter, you will learn another technique that also works in seconds.

Morphine for your brain: the SSBB technique

Don't worry, I won't send you to the dealer around the corner. Scientists have found that meditation releases the body's own morphine. Meditation works against pain and is very relaxing. The micro-technique you will discover in this chapter works like a meditation only in a very short time. Faster than you can eat a KitKat bar, you will be relaxed with this meditation. In the following, I present you this great and very effective technique to get into the here and now and to calm your amygdala. The technique is called SSBB and stands for "Stop, Smile, Breath, Be".[1]

---

[1] Zimberg (2016): *Stop Smile Breath Be – A guide to Awaken to Your True-OneSelf – The 1 Minute Mindfullness Meditation to Break Free of Stress, Fear, or Sadness to Experience Inner-*

SSBB – "Stop-Smile-Breath-Be"

Goal: Relaxation

Technique

Step 1. Stop! Stop everything. When you're in thought, stop. That doesn't mean if you're driving that you should stop the car. If you are listening to music, you do not need to turn it off. But stop your thoughts for a moment and become aware of your surroundings. Stop and pause.

Step 2. Smile! Smile broadly so that your teeth are visible. It doesn't matter if you feel like smiling. The smile can be artificial. No problem! Just smile.

Step 3. Breathe! Breathe deeply into your stomach and direct your attention to it. Follow your breath with your attention. One breath is enough.

Step 4. Be! You're here right now, right? You are. Focus your attention on your sense of being for 10 seconds.

How long? How often? The whole technique takes about 30 seconds. Do it several times a day.

Peace and Happiness.

Tips & Tricks

- **SSBBx3:** If you have some time, do the technique three times in a row. This increases the effect.

- **"Be!"** What does that mean? This step causes the most confusion. Where exactly is my feeling of being? How do I find it? Is it my body sensation? Right now, you're here. You exist, you are. You can't say you're not. You don't even have to think, you know with certainty that you are, that you exist. Nevertheless, it is difficult to say exactly where this feeling is. That's because the mind can't believe it. Just do it without thinking. You can't go wrong. Intuitively focus your attention on the feeling of being. Your mind will perhaps complain: "Where is this feeling? You're doing it wrong!" Don't pay any attention to him. If you just do it, you can't do anything wrong.

- **"Be!"** An alternative. Many find it difficult to focus their attention on their feelings. We all know that we are there and exist, but it seems difficult to focus attention on this. That's why I'm introducing you to an alternative. Close your eyes and feel into your body. Focus your attention on your right hand. Do you feel the slight tingling

and vibrating? Walk through your whole body. Everywhere you will feel these vibrations and tingling. Eckhard Tolle calls this the "inner" body. This is the alternative. Focus your attention on your energetic body. You are welcome to listen to a guided meditation on YouTube.
https://www.youtube.com/watch?v=7oL8Nqkbjdo

- **SSBB is an ultra-quick meditation.** This technique has a relaxing effect and stops your stressful thoughts. It works like a meditation. You will rapidly feel the effect.

In a Nutshell

- The amygdala lies approximately in the middle of the brain and is the size of two almond kernels.

- In case of danger, the amygdala triggers the stress reaction of flight, fight, or freeze.

- In order to get stress under control, this stress reaction must be alleviated. This can be achieved by using either 4-7-8 breathing or the SSBB technique.

- Both techniques can be applied at any time and in any situation. The stress reaction is

36

stopped instantly.

Chapter Three
How to avoid stress
in the first place

"Man's only real enemies are his own
negative thoughts." — Albert Einstein

In this chapter...

- The prefrontal cortex evaluates situations
  and passes them on to the amygdala.

- Reducing long-term stress by changing the
  valuation is easy.

- "Flipping the Switch!" turns stress into
  strength and motivation.

- The ABCDE process gives you peace in
  every situation.

Through our genes, imprints, and experiences,
the amygdala assesses certain situations as dangerous. That was vital for our ancestors. Today,
almost all situations are not life-threatening. A
dispute with your partner is unpleasant but
doesn't really threaten our lives. Our bodyguards, the amygdala, shoot wildly, although the
VIP is not threatened at all. The chief of the bodyguards, the prefrontal cortex, can intervene. He
can make the bodyguards understand that they

don't have to shoot at every person the VIP feeds, but only at those who have a weapon. Situations are re-evaluated. As a result, the amygdala sounds the alarm much less frequently, and stress is significantly reduced.

Stress-Aikido:
Turn stress into your friend

A friend of mine is doing Aikido. One day Charles said to me, "Hey, Detlef, hit me!" You know, I'm more of a peaceful fellow, and I don't box friends just like that. He didn't let up. "Hit me! I know Aikido, nothing happens to me. Really!" So I hit him, or I tried to at least. Before I knew it, I was on my nose. I groaned. Charles grinned at me: "Aikido uses the energy of your attack for defense."

What would you say if I introduced you to a technique that uses exactly this principle? When you are under stress, a lot of energy is released. Why? Because our bodies prepare to flight, fight, or freeze. This is called stress reaction. We can use this energy with the "Flipping the switch!" technique!

The idea behind this technique explains the following quote:

"It is the lens through which our brain sees the

world that shapes our reality." — Shawn Achor

Our point of view or our mindset is critical in how we handle a situation. If we see a problem as a problem, then it is one. If we see it as a challenge, then we deal with it differently.

Benjamin works in a management consultancy. On one Friday evening, he was about to go home when his boss came in. His boss said, "Ben, I'm sorry, but we just got another job. It's an emergency. Can you manage it until tomorrow?" With these words, the boss loaded a stack of papers onto Ben's desk. Ben declared, "Wow! This will be a challenge! Give me that!" Then a smile spread on his face, and he got to work.

Needless to say, Ben never suffered from stress. He simply declared everything to be a challenge. There is something very powerful about interpreting a supposedly negative event as a challenge or an opportunity. In NLP (Neuro Linguistic Programming), this is called reframing.

Flipping the Switch! technique channels the stress-energy into something positive. It is an enormously effective way to transform a stressful situation into energy and strength.

Flipping the Switch![1]

Goal: To convert stress into strength and energy

Technique

1. Accept that there is a problem

Acknowledge the reality that there is a problem. Say to yourself, "Okay, I have a problem, but I'm going to use this problem to get stronger!" We like to deny our problems until they become so strong that they can no longer be denied. That's why you should accept that there is a problem as early as possible, whether it is that you are overwhelmed by work or that the household with two children is too much.

2. Ask yourself the question

How can I use this stress or situation to improve my circumstances and make myself stronger, today, this minute, this second?

3. How does it feel?

Pay attention to what it feels like when you decide to flip the switch. Toggling the switch is a reframing of the situation. This is a term from

---

[1] Moore, Christian. The Resilience Breakthrough: 27 Tools for Turning Adversity into Action.

the NLP. They reinterpret the situation positively. You will feel more energetic and motivated. Hope and optimism will grow. That gives you more confidence, and you'll be able to think more clearly.

How often? How long? Whenever a stressful situation arises, you can flip the switch. This can be once a week or once every ten seconds.

Tips & Tricks

- **The switch is always there.** Be aware that the switch is always there. You can use it any time you want. The switch is a new perspective that gives you strength and sees the stress situation as a challenge.

- **How can we develop a positive view?** Stress is not only negative. It also has its advantages. Stress gives us strength and energy. We can use these. In my university days, I did everything at the last minute. I left the housework for weeks and only started it two days before the deadline. Of course, I was under pressure. It was stressful. Without this pressure, however, I would not have been able to complete the work.

- **Besides, stress is a signal that there is a problem**. No matter if it is a problem of our thoughts or a real one. Stress is like a wake-up call. It is forcing us to develop new skills to deal with the situation better. Our emotional intelligence will increase. Isn't that great?

- **We have the permission to be human.** This sentence comes from Tal Ben-Shahar. He is one of the best-known representatives of Positive Psychology and a professor at Harvard. Stress is part of life. You can minimize it, but it'll show up now and then. We're only human, and we don't always have everything under control. Grief, fear, anger, and stress are part of our lives. It is wise for us to accept this. Be gentle with yourself.

- **You do not always have to perform all the steps.** The second step is the decisive one! Ask yourself the "switch flipping question." If you don't have much time or you rarely work with the technique, just take the second step. That's enough! The core is that you see the situation differently and ask yourself how you can flip the switch.

- **The prefrontal cortex works with thoughts.** It evaluates the situation differently so that the amygdala does not

classify it as dangerous. Flipping the
Switch! is a reassessment of the situation.

Flipping the Switch! technique is something very
special. On the one hand, stress is immediately
reduced when it occurs, similar to SSBB or 4-7-8
breathing. In addition, however, the attitude to
the situation is also changed. Flipping the
Switch! technique has a double effect.

In the following chapter, I will introduce you to
another very effective technique, the ABCDE
process. Its aim is to prevent stress from arising
in the first place.

Positive thinking is dead

"Positive thinking" was a big thing at the beginning of this millennium. Norman Vincent Peale,
Joseph Murphy, and Maxwell Maltz were the
pioneers. Positive thinking has many good effects, but it also has one big problem. We just
can't always think positively! I tried it myself.
Our brains are not designed for positive thinking. Our primary goal is to ensure our survival.
Negative thinking is better suited for this. Worries and fears promote our survival. But there is
good news. There is something much better than
positive thinking, and you will learn about it in
this chapter.

Most people assume that events trigger our feelings. I didn't get the job, and I'm disappointed. My boss criticized me, so I'm hurt and angry. My friend cheated on me, so I'm upset and mad. We can continue this list indefinitely. But is it really so? The clear answer is *No!* It's the *thoughts* we have about a certain event that cause our emotions. Already 2000 years ago the former slave and great philosopher Epictet realized:

"It's not the things themselves that worry us, but the ideas and opinions about things."

Epictetus was born in 50 AD. He was a slave in Rome. Life as a slave was very uncertain. He had to constantly fear being beaten or killed. His master had Epictetus' leg smashed. After that Epictetus limped. To be able to endure such a life was a challenge. Fortunately, Epictetus had access to the Stoic teachings when he was still a slave. Stoicism is a philosophical direction and is known for the fact that its philosophers are always at ease. Thus Epictetus recognized that he could also be happy as a slave, since it was not the events themselves that made him suffer, but rather his attitudes and beliefs about it. Later, Epictetus was liberated and founded his own school of philosophy. He is considered one of the greatest and most influential Stoics.

It is not the events themselves that make us suffer, but rather our attitudes and convictions about the events. Is that good or bad? It's great! It means that you are independent of external events. If you lose your job, you can still be happy. If your partner breaks up with you, you can still be content. You just need to change your attitudes and thoughts. This is much easier than changing events. It is very difficult to get your partner to continue your relationship. It is easy, however, to change your attitude about this. This is the basis of Cognitive Behavioral Therapy (CBT), a very effective form of therapy.

"Cognitive Behavioral Therapy is the most time- and cost- effective psychotherapy for depression and anxiety." — Dr. Andrew Weil

What does all this have to do with stress? Remember, stress occurs when the amygdala considers a situation to be dangerous. The important prefrontal cortical assessment of the situation plays an important role for the amygdala. The prefrontal cortex is often unhelpful. If, for example, our partner leaves us, we think, "I will never find a partner again. I'll be lonely and have no friends." At some point I will die alone, and it will take three weeks for the landlord to find my body." That's what psychologists call catastrophizing. It is understandable that the amygdala will sound the alarm when we have a big fight with our partner. Since the prefrontal cortex is catastrophic, the amygdala considers the situation to be dangerous. That is why it is important that we work with our attitudes and thoughts. If we think rationally, it will save us a lot of stress.

The ABCDE process: a discussion with ourselves

We learned above that it is not events that stress us, but rather our thoughts. Only the thoughts tell us how bad it would be if we were left by our partner. It takes our thoughts to worry about how bad it would be if we lost our job. The antidote is that we simply do not believe our thoughts! As a result, they lose their impact. So we ask our thoughts if they are true. A spoiler at this point: No, our thoughts are usually not true. We can therefore, in good faith, choose not to believe them. In the following, I will introduce you to the famous ABCDE process. In this process, you will examine whether your thoughts are true. This is the cornerstone and one of the most important techniques in Cognitive Behavioral Therapy. It is simple and very effective.

ABCDE

Goal: Dissolving stress

Technique

You go through the following steps in sequence.

A = **Activating event**: What was the triggering event? For example, I'm stuck in traffic.

B = **Beliefs**: What thoughts, convictions, and beliefs do I have for A? Especially for the beginning, it is easier to formulate your beliefs as a "should" statement. For example, "I shouldn't be stuck in traffic!"

C = **Consequences**: Which feelings and actions have occurred? For example, "I am restless and annoyed that I am stuck in traffic. I'm tense."

D = **Disputing**: Here you examine whether your beliefs are true. That is the crucial point. Is your conviction a fact and therefore provable? Take one belief after another. "Should phrases" are particularly easy to explore. You may ask:

1. Is it true? Or: Where is the proof?

2. Can I really know that it would be better if... (your wish)?

Example: To 1 "Is it true that I shouldn't be stuck in traffic?" "The reality is that I'm stuck in traffic. The idea in my head that I drive relaxed on the freeway is untrue." Or, "Where's the proof that I shouldn't be stuck in traffic?" "There is no proof. There is no law that says no one should be stuck in traffic. On the contrary, it is normal to be stuck in traffic. This happens to everyone."

"Can I really know that it would be better if I wasn't stuck in traffic?" "I do not know. To know, I would have to be able to see into the future."

E = Effective new belief: Imagine how a wise man (or woman) would react in this situation. What would Epictetus tell you or the Dalai Lama? If you have someone else in mind who is very wise for you, take them.

Example: *"Unfortunately, it happens that you are sometimes stuck in traffic jams. It's everybody. It's unpleasant, but not really bad. There's nothing I can do now. It doesn't help that I'm tense and restless. This will not cause the traffic jam to disappear. Isn't everything okay now? It's warm, I hear beautiful music. Why can't I just relax and enjoy this moment?"*

How long? How often?

Once a day for three weeks. You can work on one or more topics. But please, not too many at once. If you have internalized this process, you can use the short form of the ABCDE process: When the Activating event (A) occurs, take two deep breaths or the 4-7-8-breath and then think or say the effective beliefs.

Tips & Tricks

- **Once a day**: You can implement ABCDE as a routine. Do this process in the evening, for example.

- **Written**: Put the ABCDE process on paper. This is important. Your thoughts are more organized, and the effect is stronger. Only later, when you have really internalized the process, you can really go through it in your head. However, even then it is advisable to write it from time to time.

- **Universal**: You can analyze every thought and every conviction with this method.

To B: Cool and hot beliefs – Imagine you had an interview and didn't get the job. You think, "Well, that's too bad. I'll prepare better next time." Those are cool thoughts. They hardly create emotions. If instead you think, "Damn, I'm such a loser! I'll never get a job. I'll end up in the gutter!" These are hot beliefs. They create much stronger feelings.

For stronger beliefs you should intensify the

debate. This means that you can conduct the debate as self-talk with a loud voice and convincing body language. You can clench your fists or whatever suits the disputation. This increases the effect of it.

To C: Backward Conclusion: Often we are not aware of our thoughts. We notice the feeling, but not the previous beliefs. That doesn't matter. You can deduce your beliefs from the feelings that arise. The more intense your feelings are, the harder and more unrealistic are your beliefs.

If you feel anger, your conviction will not be: "My wife is somehow a little ill at ease." No, you'll think, "Can't she just shut up? I just want to watch TV in peace! I've been working all day, and all I want is peace! She always does that! I can't stand it!"

To D: "True" means this thing really exists." You may ask yourself, "What does a camera see?" When I think, "I'm a loser!" Are there failures? No! We may make mistakes, but that doesn't mean I'm a failure.

To D: There are a few subs-questions that you can ask yourself. You can deepen the effect or clarify the matter.

Sub-question #1: "Can I really know it would

be better for me if (your wish)?"

Sub-question #2: "Can I really know that it would be better for the other person(s) if (your wish)?"?

Sub-question #3: "Can I really know that it would be better in the long run (in 10 years) if (your wish)?"?

ABCDE in short: If you have made the process more frequent for a specific topic, you can shorten it. If the triggering event occurs, you can apply your effective beliefs directly. It is best if you breathe deeply twice or do the 4-7-8-breath and then think or express your effective convictions.

Examples of the ABCDE process

At first glance, the ABCDE process looks complicated, but with practice, you'll find out how easy it is. Here are a few examples to help you get to know the process better.

Example: Job interview

A = Activating Event: Fred goes to an interview and is rejected. This is the triggering event.

B = Beliefs: These are the thoughts, attitudes, and beliefs about the activating event. Fred thinks: "I should get the job! I shouldn't be so incapable!" Those are hot thoughts.

C = Consequences: These are the consequences of beliefs. The feelings that arise and possible actions that are triggered by the beliefs. Fred's hot convictions give rise to intense feelings. Fred will feel bad. His self-esteem is suffering, and he most likely won't reapply. These are the consequences.

D = Disputation: We examine the beliefs one by one.

"I should get the job!"

Is that true? Where's the proof? Is there any proof that Fred should get the job? No! There's no law that says Fred should get the job.

Does Fred really know that it's better if he got the job? We'll look into this right away with the sub-questions.

Sub-question # 1: Can Fred really know that it would have been better for him if he had gotten the job? No! For that, Fred would have to be able to see into the future. Maybe he will be offered a better job later, or he will realize that he doesn't like this job type at all.

Sub-question #2: Can Fred really know that it would have been better for the others if he had gotten the job? For the company that turned him down, it's obviously better he didn't get the job.

Sub-question #3: Can Fred really know that in the long run (10 years), it would have been better if he had the job? No. Ten years is a long time. Fred probably wouldn't even remember that interview.

"I shouldn't be so incapable!"

Is that true? Where's the proof? Was Fred really incapable? What exactly does it mean to be incapable? Fred would have to find out exactly what the reason was for the rejection. If Fred caused it at all, he can say more realistically that he wasn't prepared well enough.

Sub-question # 1: Can Fred really know that it would have been better for him if he had been capable? No! Maybe he wouldn't have got the job if he'd been capable. If he had gotten the job, Fred wouldn't know if it was optimal for him. Because for that, Fred would have to be able to see into the future. Maybe it would have missed a better job offer.

Sub-question #2: Can Fred really know that it would have been better for the others if he had been capable? Fred doesn't know that either.

Sub-question #3: Can Fred really know that in

the long run (10 years) it would have been better if he had been capable? No. Ten years is a long time. Probably he will get another and better job.

E = Effective new philosophy: "Too bad I would have liked the job, but there are enough other vacancies. The fact that I did not receive this position says nothing about me as a person. I may have made a mistake, though."

Believe it or not, we all think alike. Beliefs repeat themselves and can be divided into 11 categories. These I would like to introduce to you in the following.

Categories of beliefs

1st Belief: *"I must be loved and approved by every important person around me. Otherwise, it's horrible."*

Examples: "I'm afraid to ask for a date."

"I couldn't bear it if he were angry with me."

"I would do anything for that person!"

This conviction is very common. Women are more susceptible to these thoughts.

Effective Belief: I have no magical power over other people, I cannot force them to love or agree with me. It happens that I'm not loved or that I don't get approval. This has nothing to do with me and my value.

2nd Belief: *"If someone else behaves badly or unfairly, then he must be reprimanded or punished, because he is a bad or a depraved person."*

Examples: "It's all your fault!"

"You shouldn't have done that to me!"

"I'll get back at him!"

"My parents should have been fair. I wouldn't be in this mess!"

Effective Belief: Certain acts are inappropriate or antisocial. This does not mean that the whole person is bad or condemnable. It's just his act. This often happens out of personal suffering or ignorance.

3rd Belief: *"It's terrible when things aren't what I want them to be!"*

Examples: "I don't want to be treated unfairly!"

"I keep running after you and cleaning up!"

"I don't have any more time for myself!"

"I can't do without it!"

The examples are unfinished sentences. This is

based on the conclusion that things should be different. It's very common. Very often, when we suffer, it is because we want it to be different. This is nothing bad in itself, it is permissible that we want to change situations. It only becomes problematic if it is not allowed. That is, when it is implicitly said that it is bad or horrible as it is.

Effective Belief: It's a pity it's not the way we'd like it to be. But that's life. Actually, it's almost never the way we'd like it to be. It is wise to accept this. This does not mean that we cannot try to change it but out of an inner peace.

4th Belief: *"I should be very afraid of events that are uncertain or potentially dangerous."*

Examples: "I can't think of anything else."

"It could happen!"

"You want me to get on a horse?"

"But how can I be sure it won't happen?"

This belief is based on the quest for security in life. Unfortunately, life is uncertain. We have no control. We are thus facing an additional problem: Because we are not only upset when the event actually happens, but even before it happens. The worries and fears in advance are useless.

Effective Belief: It is better to prepare yourself properly and face the danger. It's no use whining about it.

5th Belief: *"I am worthless if I am not thoroughly competent and always up to any situation, and if I am not successful at all times, or at least most of the time in one of the more important areas."*

Examples: "What an idiot I am!"

"I shouldn't have yelled at the kids!"

"I'm not intelligent enough to study."

"I shouldn't have had an orgasm so quickly."

This belief is very widespread. It's more likely to affect men. The person concerned thinks he is a failure if he has failed on a particular matter.

Effective Belief: Nobody can do everything all the time. That's not possible. Everyone makes mistakes and has weaknesses. Am I God that I expect something like this from myself?

6th Belief: *"There must be a perfect solution to this problem. I must be sure and have complete control over things."*

Examples: "I just can't make a decision."

"There must be a better way."

"Doctor, do you think you can tell me what to do?"

"But how can I be sure?"

This belief has two irrational building blocks. On the one hand, we believe that there is a perfect solution and that we must find it. If we don't find it, it's bad. On the other hand, we strive for complete control and safety. There isn't any of either. We have very limited control over life. This conviction can also apply to other people who cannot offer a perfect solution. This can then manifest itself in anger and rage.

We don't have as much control as we think. The great philosopher Epictetus said about 2000 years ago:

"Some things are in our power, but others are not. In our power are judgments, aspirations, desire, and distraction: in a word, everything that is the product of our will. Not in our power are our body, possessions, honor, position, and all that is not our work." — *Epictetus*

A strong quote from a great philosopher. If you are annoyed about other people's behavior, this is very understandable, but not helpful. You have no control over other people's behavior, so you can relax. The same applies to the weather, whether you are stuck in traffic, or become ill. It's out of your power.

Effective Belief: Our world and our lives are uncertain and insecure. Nevertheless, it can be enjoyed.

7th Belief: *"The world should be fair and even-handed."*

Examples: "How could she do this to me?"

"Why does something like this always happen to me?"

"You had no right to fire me."

"You can't tell me what to do."

We all have to learn that life is sometimes unfair and inequitable, like a colleague who performs less than us is promoted before us. You get taken down by the boss even though you didn't make a mistake. I'm sure you know many other examples from your own life. "The world should be fair" is a pious wish, but unfortunately, it is not reality.

Effective Belief: It would be nice if the world were fair. Unfortunately, it's not like that. It is wise to accept this.

8th Belief: *"I should be able to live comfortably*

and without suffering all the time."

Examples: "It's just too heavy."

"But I don't like it."

"I can't stand it."

"What, I should go to the dentist? That hurts too much."

This belief is a sign of low frustration tolerance and often leads to addictions and behavioral excesses or at least to nagging. Fear of inconvenience prevents us from achieving long-term goals.

Effective Belief: It would be nice if I never had to suffer. Unfortunately, life isn't like that. I decide to endure inconvenience even if I don't like it.

9th Belief: *"I could lose my mind, and that would be unbearable."*

Examples: "I can't even think straight anymore."

"I'm so afraid that I can't control myself."

"I'm so afraid to get mad!"

"Is this normal?"

The fear of going mad is a widespread fear. We

have the most adventurous ideas about psychiatry. We think we're going to get locked up in a loony bin.

Effective Belief: An emotional disorder is certainly nothing pleasant, but it is hardly unbearable.

10th Belief: *"Emotional suffering comes from the outside, and I have few possibilities to control or change my feelings."*

Examples*:* "I'll be completely destroyed when she leaves me."

"He makes me so angry."

"If you stopped nagging me, I could change."

"If I got this job, I'd be happy."

The idea that our feelings depend solely on external circumstances is very common. But we now know that this is not true. Our beliefs cause our feelings. The number ten conviction makes us a victim Our circumstances make us suffer and often we cannot change the circumstances. This is an excuse and leads us to remain in our emotional suffering.

Effective Belief: Suffering is caused by our views of things and our beliefs, not by the situation itself. That's great, because we don't have to suffer anymore.

11th Belief: *"The cause of my present problems lies in my past. Because past events have had a tremendous influence on me, they will continue to do so in the future."*

Example: "Well, I was brought up the same way."

"I had a bad childhood."

"In reality, it's my mother's fault. She made me who I am."

This conviction implies that we cannot change. We can't do anything because the past has caused our present world of emotions. That is why it is important to discuss this conviction.

Effective Belief: Where is the proof of this conviction? I can learn from past experiences and change.

All your beliefs fall into one or more of the categories. Especially at the beginning, when we work with this method it can be helpful to work with it. It gives you hints as to what exactly is wrong with your conviction and what your effective belief may look like. You don't necessarily have to work with the categories, but if you're stuck, just have a look.

Another example

Let's look at another example:

"My boss should praise and appreciate me more!"

A: Bob has achieved a great success in his work. His boss says nothing about it.

B: Bob thinks, "My boss should praise and appreciate me more!"

C: Bob is angry and demotivated.

D: It is belief one, three, or seven.

1. Is it true? I don't know if he doesn't acknowledge me, because I'd have to be able to read his mind. He appreciates me because he pays my salary. That's worth a lot!

2. Can I know it would be better for me? I can't know. Praise is good, but it's not really important.
Can I know it would be better for him? Probably not for my boss, because otherwise he would. He's probably too busy.
In the long run? Who knows what's going to happen in 10 years? Maybe I have a completely different position.

E: What my boss does is out of my power. He

recognizes my achievements by paying me. It would be nice if he praised me, but it's my decision if I consider it important.

You are free in the disputation, there are no fixed rules. You can be creative. The important thing is that you feel better with the disputation. But don't fool yourself. Disputation is about truth. Do not replace your beliefs from B with beliefs that are equally untrue. For example, "I am the greatest! I am perfect! That's why I don't need any credit." These beliefs make you feel better, but it's only short-term, since you will soon realize that these convictions are not true either. Reality always wins.

Would you like to know more? The following books and links are real pearls.

Ellis (2006). *How To Stubbornly Refuse To Make Yourself Miserable About Anything – Yes, Anything.* Link: https://amzn.to/2lYG1TR
This book is from Dr. Albert Ellis. He is one of the founders of cognitive behavioral therapy. This book will change your life.

Katie, Byron (2008). *Loving What Is: How Four Questions Can Change Your Life.* Link: https://amzn.to/2MWQ1s7
This book is a great read. However, it does not

explain the ABCDE model, but a very similar one called TheWork. Although it is not quite the same, you can learn a lot from this book as it is excellently explained. Some of the examples and approaches for this book have been taken from it.

On YouTube, there are great videos on this topic. Just enter "Albert Ellis, REBT or Byron Katie." Then you will receive a variety of suggestions.

In a Nutshell

- The prefrontal cortex is the boss. It thinks logically and solves problems.

- It assesses situations and transmits this information to the amygdala. During her childhood, the amygdala learned to regard harmless situations as dangerous.

- Fortunately, this process can be undone. The prefrontal cortex re-evaluates situations and passes this on to the amygdala. Since fewer situations are considered dangerous, the amygdala is less likely to trigger the stress reaction.

- So we are talking about revaluations. That is why you have learned techniques in this chapter that work with thoughts and beliefs.

- The technique of "Flipping the Switch!" is rather situational.

- The ABCDE process is very profound and should be written.

Chapter Four
The 4-step formula

"Happiness can't be enforced, but it likes persistent people." — Anonymous

In this chapter...

- The 4-step formula eliminates stress
- Every problem has an internal and external front.
- The ABCDE+1 as a core
- Provide variety

You have learned effective techniques to say goodbye to your stress once and for all. The 4-step formula puts everything into a simple step-by-step guide. It has been proven, and you will see how your stress is relieved.

Let's take a closer look at this.

Step 1: Find the causes of your stress and eliminate them

Let's look at a short example.

Fabian has been married for 12 years. From his point of view, his wife Liz is always nagging him, and they argue a lot. He finds his relationship stressful. He can now work on the inner

and outer front of the problem:

- **Inner front** means that Fabian is working on his inner handling. For example, he could apply the ABCDE model and review and dispute his beliefs. He could also use the "Flipping the Switch!" technique to see quarrels as challenges. This would give him strength.

- **Outer front**: This is Fabian trying to change the outer circumstances. If a recurring complaint of his wife is that he brings out the trash bin too late, he might try to empty the bin more often. Another possibility to work on the outer front is that Fabian separates from his wife.

If there is a problem, we can always work on both fronts. If you have stress at work, you can learn to deal with it better with the help of the ABCDE process. Often this can be enough. However, it never hurts to check whether you can also improve the external situation.

Karl was often late. This was a constant stress factor, especially in his work. He put himself under a lot of pressure and got under stress.

- **Inner Front**: On the one hand, he looked at the beliefs that led him to be late. Secondly, with the help of the ABCDE process, he worked to be at peace with being late.

- **Outer front**: Karl trained to leave on time. He set an alarm on his cell phone. In addition, he got up 10 minutes earlier every morning. Karl thus managed to be much more punctual.

The first step is the diagnosis. Often we are not even aware of the situations that cause stress.

1. Be a stress detective: Identify your stress-inducing situations. Take a piece of paper and write down situations in which you feel stressed. Find at least three situations. In the quiz under the following link you will get an initial assessment in which areas of your life stress triggers can be found: *https://bit.ly/2u3sQp3* Under the following link you will find common triggers of stress: *https://wb.md/2yP49zq*.

I have a confession to make. I've read a lot of self-help books. Whenever I had to write something down, like my beliefs or something, I would put the book aside. That was too much trouble. You may also be tempted to do what I did. Don't do it! Write down the stressful situations and follow the 4-step formula. Writing it down is really quick. Do it by feel. You can still change the list later. It's worth it! Your life may well improve! If it's hard for you, just write down one situation. Just get started!

2. Rankings: Think about the level of stress in the individual situations. Assess them on a stress scale:

0 = not at all stressful and completely neutral,

.

.

10 = maximum stressful situation.

Now create a ranking list. The most stressful situation is at the top, the least stressful situation at the bottom.

3. Actions: Start with the situation that causes you the most stress. Consider how you can improve the outer front. Can you eliminate external stressors? Think about what you can do. Try to find three actions each.

This is what a ranking could look like.

stress trigger	stress level	possible actions
Disputes with partner	8	1. Going to Couples Therapy 2. Improve communication 3. Separation
Delays to work	6	1. Wake up 10 minutes earlier 2. Set the alarm 3. Set up flextime at work
Presentations for customers	6	1. Visit workshop for presentations 2. Regular relaxation exercises 3. Ask boss for relief

The more precisely you describe the situation, the better. If you list "Stress at work," this is too general. Identify exactly what is stressing you. The more precise the situation, the easier it is to find countermeasures. If presentations cause stress for you, you can find specific solutions. On the other hand, with "Stress at work," you're taking a shot in the dark.

Your task now is to try to implement the actions. This can significantly reduce your stress.

2. Step: ABCDE+1

In this book, we focus on the inner front. Why? Often external circumstances cannot be changed or are not to the complete satisfaction. Experience shows that an improvement of the external circumstances alleviates the stress, but only very rarely dissolves it completely. In fact, the inner front is more important and powerful than the outer front. External circumstances are difficult to influence, but you can change your thinking much more easily.

Think of the great philosopher and slave Epictetus. He was trapped in a very painful situation. He was a slave and at the mercy of his master at all times. He could be abused or even killed at any time. He couldn't change anything on the outer front. He found peace by working exclusively on the internal front. Amazing! His situation was so terrible, but he found peace with it only by changing his beliefs and thoughts. We can, too!

Apply the ABCDE process once a day for three weeks. You will see how relaxed your life can become. It's enough if you only do it for a few minutes, but it has to be in writing. Thoughts are fleeting and difficult to capture. That is why we drag them to the light of day by writing them down. This makes us really aware of our thoughts. We see them in black and white on our paper. Many people are amazed at the strange and irrational thoughts they have. Others wonder how negative and mean the voice in their head is.

"It was at that moment, when I was in bed at night, realizing for the first time that the voice in my head - the constant commentary that has dominated my consciousness since I can remember - was some kind of asshole."
— Dan Harris

The ABCDE process influences the prefrontal cortex. We apply the ABCDE process when we are not under stress. This changes the assessment of a situation.

However, it is also important to alleviate the stress in the **acute stress** situation itself. Use another technique: Choose the one that is easiest for you and the one that works best for you. You can choose between 4-7-8-breathing and SSBB-technique. These are acute techniques that act directly on the amygdala. All are very effective and can be used without much effort.

3. Step: Quick-ABCDE and variety

After three weeks you can simplify your practice.

Short ABCDE: You can now use the ABCDE process in everyday life whenever it is necessary. You don't have to do this in writing. We usually don't have time for that. In the short version, it is sufficient to express your effective beliefs. This is very powerful. You interrupt your negative self-talk and say to yourself (internally or out loud) your effective convictions. It's much more effective than just stopping your thoughts. You have already written the ABCDE process for all situations, so that the short variant is sufficient.

Example: Suppose you're stressed because you're late again. Your effective belief is: "If I stress, I won't get there any faster. If I'm a few minutes late, it's not optimal, but it's not bad either. My health is more important to me, and so I can relax."

Breathing: Before using the short ABCDE, breathe in and out deeply twice to reduce acute stress.

One to three times in writing: After three weeks, you are already very familiar with the ABCDE process. It is now sufficient to write the long process only one to three times a week.

A tip: Vary your techniques. Our brains like variety. Try another technique. If you have practiced the SSBB so far, try the 4-7-8 breath. You can also use the "Flipping the Switch!" technique in acute situations. Breathe in and out twice deeply into your stomach. Then flip the switch.

Step 4: Herbal remedies and supplements

Use the herbs and supplements from the bonus chapter right from the start. These are easy to implement that can reduce your stress without any effort. They are very well tolerated and support your process effortlessly.

In a Nutshell

- The techniques in this book are very effective. But if we don't use them, they're of no use to us.

- The 4-step formula tells you exactly what you can do and when.

- Be a detective. Find the causes of your stress and eliminate them.

- Practice the techniques that suit you, but always include the ABCDE process.

- Use the power of herbal remedies and supplements.

Bonus: How to stay tuned

"A journey of a thousand miles begins with the first step." — Lao Tse

In this chapter...

- Persistence is the be-all and end-all of success.

- How to keep it rolling in the long term with the help of memory apps, solar flare technology, and other techniques

I have not yet mentioned the most important building block for you to relieve your stress. You must use the techniques described here. I care about your happiness, so I'll give you a few hints and hacks on how to use the techniques.

Simple tricks on micro tactics

What are micro-tactics in this book? It's the SSBB, the 4-7-8-breathing, and "Flipping the Switch!" These techniques cost us hardly any time and we can apply them in everyday life at any time. That's why it is called micro tactics. The main problem with these techniques is that we easily forget them. If we plan to jog for 30 minutes once a day, we will not forget this. But if we plan to practice SSBB five times a day, this can be quickly forgotten. For this there are several possible solutions:

Reminder app: There are some apps that either remind at certain times of the day or at certain intervals. I use ReDo Reminder for Android. This app certainly won't win a beauty prize, but it's practical and easy to use. With this app, you can remember the techniques.

Linking with existing habits: One possibility is to link the techniques with other habits. You can even associate them with negative habits. In this case, it makes sense to link the techniques with stressful situations. For example, every time your partner nags you, you can do the 4-7-8 breath. You can also associate other habits or situations. In the morning, immediately after waking up, do an SSBB. Every time you want to eat something sweet, practice 4-7-8 breathing first. Think about what suits you best.

Visualization of the ideal day: Furthermore, a very effective technique is to visualize your ideal day. You can do that right after you wake up while you're still in bed, provided you're not too drowsy. If you are too sleepy, drink a large glass of water or shower first.

Visualization of the ideal day

Goal: Build up motivation and remember

Technique:
Imagine how you make the techniques you have planned for this day with joy. For example, if you are planning to use SSBB, imagine how you will practice it with joy.

How long? How often? Daily in the morning for 2 - 3 minutes.

Tips & Tricks

- **Visualize links**: For example, you plan on practicing 4-7-8 breathing after 20 minutes of watching TV after going to the bathroom and before eating something. Imagine watching TV after 20 minutes, sitting upright and performing the 4-7-8-breath. Imagine how you do your breathing after your toilet and before you eat something.

- **Successful**: Imagine how you enjoy your techniques and are successful.

- **No limits**: You can also visualize other things. Maybe you're having a conversation with your boss, which is stressing you out. Imagine how this conversation works optimally. You can imagine what you do when your boss criticizes you. If you have an appointment with a dentist, you can imagine how relaxed you are about the situation. There are no limits to the possibilities that you can use.

Hacks to the ABCDE process

Congratulations! If you have made it this far, you've already come a long way. Nevertheless, it's not always easy to keep up. Therefore, the few tips below can give you a boost in motivation:

Solar flare technique: The special thing about a solar flare is that it starts very small but then becomes mind-blowingly big. You can use this principle by taking it upon yourself to start with only one tiny activity. For example, in the ABCDE process, you decide to write only one line. The idea is that the beginning is hard and often keeps us from doing anything at all. If we plan to jog for 45 minutes, it is much harder for us to start than if we plan to run for only two minutes. Once we have started, however, we will probably continue. Try it out. You will be surprised how well the technique works.

Commit yourself with StickK.com: This page is about giving you an additional motivation boost to build habits. For example, you want to start jogging every day, beginning tomorrow. You have the possibility to deposit money at StickK.com. You lose your money if you don't jog every day. This can be very motivating. It should be an amount that hurts if you lose it. So not USD $5, but rather USD $200. The StikK.com website is well done. They also have other ways to commit. Take a look at the page. It's worth it.

Seinfeld Calendar and TrackerApp: The idea goes back to comedian Jerry Seinfeld. He was committed to inventing a new joke every day. Once he had done that, he made a big red cross in his calendar. He said that he mustn't break the chain. So not a day goes by without a big red cross. Not wanting to break the chain can be very motivating. You are welcome to use a calendar, but an app also works. There are several TrackerApps, a simple app that is a goal and habit tracker. It is easy to use, and it works.

Reward yourself: You can reward yourself when you reach a milestone. For example, if you have successfully completed the ABCDE process in writing for three weeks, enjoy a massage. You can also reward yourself with little things. If you have visualized the ideal day, have a tasty breakfast as a reward. Rewards are a great tool to positively strengthen habits. We tend to criticize ourselves when we have not achieved something. It is better to reward ourselves when we have done something good. This strengthens our self-esteem.

In a Nutshell

- The 4-7-8 breath, the SSBB-technique, and the "Flipping the Switch!" technique are always applicable in everyday life. The problem with these techniques is that they are quickly forgotten.

- **Solutions**: Use a reminder app, link the techniques with existing habits, or practice the exercise of visualizing the ideal day.

- The ABCDE process is more complex because it should be written in the first three weeks. The problem is that you need more motivation to keep up.

- **Solution**: Use the solar flare technique, the Seinfeld calendar, or StikK.com.

Bonus:
Herbal remedies and supplements

"Dear God! Can you make the vitamins from the spinach go into the custard?" —
Anonymous

In this chapter...

- The best herbal remedies for stress

- Supplements to reduce stress

So far, you've learned mental techniques. They are extremely effective. However, you can support these techniques with herbal remedies and dietary supplements. First, I'd like to introduce you to some herbal products.

Ginseng

There are a number of studies on the effects of ginseng. Proven effects include performance enhancement, antidepressant, nerve strengthening, improvement of the immune system and potency, and a positive effect on the liver. Ginseng also has a regulating effect on blood sugar levels and blood lipids. Ginseng is slightly stimulating.

St. John's Wort

This plant is the best studied herbal remedy. It

has a mood-lifting effect and thus works against mild-to-moderate depression. The usual dose is 300 milligrams, three times daily. However, the herb works slowly. The full effect can only be felt after two months of continuous use.

Roseroot (Rhodiola)

If you have mild to moderate depression or feel lacking in energy, you can take roseroot. Studies have confirmed that roseroot has a significant anti-depressive effect in mild and moderate depression. Dr. Weil, one of the leading experts in happiness research, recommends that you take 100 milligrams twice a day, in the morning and early afternoon. Taken too late, it can cause sleep problems. You can increase the dose to 200 milligrams three times daily, but again, be careful not to take it too late. Negative effects with other drugs have hardly been investigated, so you should ask your doctor here.

Ashwagandha

Studies have shown that Ashwagandha alleviates fears and has a mood-lifting effect. Dr. Low Dog, one of the leading experts in the field of herbal medicine, recommends taking 300-500 milligrams of this plant two to three times a day. It has no sedating effect and can be taken during the day. According to Dr. Low Dog, Ashwagandha is one of the most effective herbal remedies against chronic stress, sleep problems, and lack of energy.

Valeriana

This healing root has a long and successful history. It has a sleep-inducing and anti-anxiety effect. There is no danger of addiction. Use standardized valerian extract with 0.8% valerian acid. Take 250 milligrams with meals up to three times daily.

Kava

Kava works very well against anxiety. Studies have shown that kava works just as well against anxiety as benzodiazepines. There are rare reports that there are side effects on the liver. That's why people with liver damage should avoid this plant. Alcohol or antidepressants can be addictive. Otherwise, the root is safe. Dr. Weil recommends kava extract standardized to 30% kavapyrone. You take this up to three times daily in a dose of 100 or 200 milligrams. It works quickly against anxiety. Do not take it for more than a few months.

Herbal remedies work well against stress and have hardly any side effects. But you can also counteract stress with dietary supplements. The following supplements are effective against stress:

- B-complex vitamins
- Vitamin C
- Zinc
- Magnesium

In a Nutshell

- Valerian and Kava work well against fear.
- Ginseng, Roseroot, and St. John's Wort are natural antidepressants.
- Ashwagandha has both mood-lifting and anti-anxiety effects.

Summary

"Look up the last pages of a book if you can't wait for the finale. Reality doesn't allow it."
— Joachim Panten

Stress is an illusion. Who would have thought it? We can use this statement to combat stress in the long term, as we now evaluate stress-inducing situations differently. In this book, you have learned the 4-step formula. It will considerably reduce your stress with the help of a few techniques.

Technique	Application	Goal	Effort	Support
4-7-8 breath	Acute stress, 2 x daily	Amygdala calm, relieve acute stress	Low	Visualization of the ideal day, ReDo Reminder, Linking
SSBB	Acute stress	Amygdala calm, relieve acute stress	Low	Visualization of the ideal day, ReDo Reminder, Linking
Flipping the Switch!	Several times a day	Influence prefrontal cortex, prevent stress	Low	Visualization of the ideal day, ReDo Reminder, Linking
ABCDE	1 x daily for 3 weeks, then several times a day	Influence prefrontal cortex, prevent stress	Moderate	Solar flare technique, StikK.com, Seinfeld calendar

We can relieve stress acutely and fight it in the long term.

1. Reduce acute stress reaction: That is, we calm the amygdala with the help of 4-7-8 breath or the SSBB technique.

2. Tackling the root cause of the stress problem: We influence the prefrontal cortex so that it re-evaluates situations and passes them on to the amygdala. As a result, the amygdala sounds the alarm less frequently. The techniques of "Flipping the switch!" and the ABCDE process are highly effective.

Congratulations on reading this far! I hope you've enjoyed it. It is important to me that you reduce your stress, so I appeal to you to use the techniques. I know from my own experience how difficult it is to overcome the inner, weaker self and apply something in the long term. Unfortunately, this is the work we must do if we want to improve our lives. The techniques in this book can improve your life enormously! I wish you luck, low stress, and much joy in your life!

Free Gift

"The clearest sign of wisdom is a consistently good mood." — Michel de Montaigne

As a thank you, I would like to give you a gift! Here's my book "**18 Surprising Good-Mood Tips**" (52 pages). You can download it at the following link:

http://detlefbeeker.de/gift/

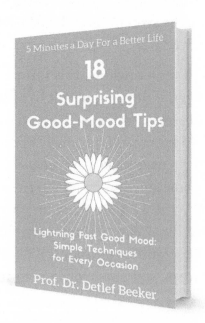

Do you remember the first time you fell in love? Wasn't everything suddenly nice? How wonderful the blue sky looked, with its white clouds. Even rain you could enjoy. What if you could have this lovely mood all the time?

In this book, you will learn:

- **Body parts** to press to relieve stress and improve your mood and health

- Proven mental tactics that will put you in a good mood in seconds

- Secret Yoga techniques that will easily increase your good mood

- The unknown piece of music is scientifically proven to be the best stress reducer

- What you can learn from James Bond and how it gives you relaxation and self-confidence

- How you can relax in 10 seconds

- Practice this mind-boggling technique and get fresh and vitalized.

- The best apps to relieve your stress and give you relaxation and serenity

- The Fidget Cube and how it works

- Bonus: The new generation of good mood techniques

- ... and much more

Download this book NOW for **free,** so that you'll be guaranteed more joy, serenity, and happiness with the help of the best techniques.

http://detlefbeeker.de/gift/

You belong to extraordinary 3.2%

"Not the beginning is rewarded but only the perseverance."

Do you hear the applause? You deserve it. Why? Because only 10% of readers go beyond the first chapter of a book, and you've read the whole book! So you bring things to an end - an important skill. Also, you are among the special groups of readers who read self-help books. Only 32% do so. By the way, we have something in common. I love self-help books too! That together, you belong to selected 3.2%. Well, if that is not worth the applause!

I put a lot of passion into this book. That's why I'm glad that you found it so interesting to read. It gives me the courage to ask you for a small favor: It costs you nothing, but would help me enormously: **Would you take a minute or two of your time and write a quick review?** Two or three short sentences are enough. You can write them on the book page

https://amzn.to/2N8wWmC

Maybe it seems unimportant, but every single review counts. Your positive review helps me continue to work as an independent author and write books that help people.

Thank you so much!

Yours sincerely

Detlef Beeker

Website of the author: http://detlefbeeker.de/en

PS: If you do not like the book, please let me know. Any kind of feedback is valuable to me. Just write me an email to detlef@detlefbeeker.de.

About the series
"5 Minutes for a Better Life."

"Success is the sum of small efforts, repeated day in and day out." — R. Collier

This quote is the philosophy of this series. We don't have to do much; small actions can be enough. However, we should note the following:

- On the other hand, we must apply them in the long term. We need perseverance.

- On the other hand, we should choose the actions wisely. This is what the *Pareto principle* tells us:

Pareto principle*: 20% of the effort leads to 80% of the result. This is an empirical law, which was discovered by Vilfredo Pareto. For example, 80% of a company's revenue is generated by 20% of its customers.*

Isn't that great? We have to choose the means we use cleverly. So we can achieve 80% of the desired result with little effort. We can then come up with a winning formula:

Success = skillful, small actions + persistence

This formula is the basis of the series "Five Minutes Daily for a Better Life." And yes, it is possible. Change doesn't always have to be time-consuming. Science used to think that you have to do sports for at least three hours a week to promote good health. Today we know that 30 minutes a week is enough if you train skillfully. That's not even up to five minutes a day.

Disclaimer and Imprint

are excluded in general, unless there is evidence of willful intent or gross negligence on the part of the author. This book is not a substitute for the medical and professional advice and support. This book refers to contents of the third party. The author hereby, expressly declares that at the time the links were created, no illegal content was recognizable on the linked pages. The author has no influence on the linked content. The author, therefore, dissociates himself from all contents of all linked pages which were changed after the link was set up. For illegal, incorrect or incomplete contents and especially for damages resulting from the use or non-use of such information, only the provider of the page to which reference was made is liable, but not the author of this book.

Detlef Beeker

Made in the USA
Coppell, TX
26 July 2021

59489856R00059